K. G. C.

AN
AUTHENTIC EXPOSITION
OF THE
ORIGIN, OBJECTS, AND SECRET WORK OF THE ORGANIZATION KNOWN AS THE
KNIGHTS OF THE GOLDEN CIRCLE.

[Published by the U. S National U. C.— February 1862.]

The loyal people of the United States have long been aware of the existence in this country, and especially in the Southern States, of various secret organizations having for their object the "Americanization" of some of our weaker neighbors beyond the Southern limits of our domain, and the aggrandizement of their leaders and members through the forcible acquisition of the territory, and the subversion of the governments of the Central American States and Mexico. Of this character was the order of the LONE STAR, under whose auspices men and means were raised for the LOPEZ raids upon the Island of Cuba, in the years 1850 and 1851, and for the subsequent forays into the Central American States under the leadership of the "grey-eyed man of destiny," WILLIAM WALKER. These hostile designs upon the territory of our Southern neighbors having failed, the order fell into disrepute, and its secrets were exposed and burlesqued by the "SONS OF MALTA."

This order of the LONE STAR, was a branch of that now known as the K. G. C., if indeed it was not identical with it. Probably thousands of our fellow-citizens, North and South, who were once familiar with the secret work of the order of the LONE STAR, will be able to discern the old land-marks throughout the exposition contained in these pages. We are assured by an intelligent gentleman, once a member of this organization, that in its earlier history it had no designs hostile to our own Government and people; but that its sole object was the acquisition of foreign territory by force of arms, the introduction of immigrants from the Southern States, who should seize upon and possess the soil, and reduce the natives to the condition of slaves, or expel them from the country at the point of the bayonet. These grand schemes failed for the time, and the surviving members of this band of land pirates soon found work at home.

Of the K. G. C., a writer in the *Continental Monthly*, for January, 1862, says:—"This organization, which was instituted by John C. Calhoun, William L. Porcher, and others, as far back as 1835, had for its sole object the dissolution of the Union, and the establishment of a Southern Empire;—Empire is the word, not Confederacy or Republic;—and it was solely by means of its secret, but powerful machinery, that the Southern States were plunged into revolution, in defiance of the will of a majority of their voting population. Nearly every man of influence at the South, (and many a pretended Union man at the North,) is a member of this organization, and sworn, *under the penalty of assassination*, to labor 'in season and out of season, by fair means and by foul, at all times and on all occasions,' for the accomplishment of its object."

Upon what evidence the above statement in regard to the agency of Messrs. Calhoun and Porcher in the foundation of this organization is made, we know not;

Entered, according to Act of Congress, February 20, 1862, in the Clerk's Office of the District Court for the District of Kentucky.

but there can be no reasonable doubt that these men and their associates did resort to secret and powerful means for the spread of their views, and for the instruction of the public mind of the South in those doctrines of Disunion and Treason which they originated. Through these means, and especially by the agency of the K. G. C., "the Southern mind has been educated and the Southern heart fired," persistently and thoroughly, for a long series of years, until the hopes of the arch traitors were in part realized by the inauguration of civil war, on the 12th of April, 1861, by that fatal shot for the South, the firing of the first gun at Fort Sumpter!

Since the commencement of the internal dissensions in the United States, which culminated in the Great Rebellion of 1861-2, this treasonable organization has acquired new strength, and become widely disseminated throughout the length and breadth of our land, embracing within its circle many thousands of disloyal men, who are secretly conspiring against the rights and liberties of our people. Men of all grades in society, from the lordly banker and merchant, the eloquent statesman and the ambitious politician, down to the lowest ruffian and assassin who infests the purlieus of our cities, are believed to be connected with this organization: their object being the advancement of their own ends, whatever they may be, even at the sacrifice of our government, our rights, our liberties, and even our existence as a great and powerful nation. Indeed, the cardinal object of this conspiracy seems to be the utter destruction of the Great Republic, and the establishment upon its ruins, of a military despotism, or of an oligarchy, wherein the rich may lord it over the poor, making the laws which shall govern the "mud-sills of society," and dictating the terms upon which the great mass of the people of this broad land shall be permitted to exist.

There is good reason to believe that the chief seat of the power of the K. G. C. has recently been transferred from the Southern States to Canada, and that it has powerful allies among the nobility, bankers and merchants of England. Having accomplished its great design at the South, by arousing the people to the fighting point, it leaves them in the hands of the military despots, who rule them with a rod of iron, joins hands with our foreign foes, and seeks, by the foulest secret means, the overthrow of our liberties. Our foreign enemies are banded together in this infamous league, by tens of thousands, and are vigorously at work, night and day, "at all times and all seasons, by fair means and by foul," to accomplish the fulfilment of their long cherished hopes, and oft repeated predictions of the downfall of our Republican form of government, the dismemberment of our Union, and the utter destruction of this last and greatest home of freedom for the oppressed nations of the old world.

Men of America! Who love your country with all its glorious memories, and all its bright prospects of future greatness, whose fathers freely shed their blood to secure to you and to your children the blessings of civil and religious liberty, THESE ARE FACTS! and you shall be convinced of them. Your enemies are secretly at work in your very midst, and are in conspiracy with foreign emissaries to deprive you of the blessings which you have ever enjoyed under your paternal government, and for the maintenance of which you may be compelled yet again to peril your lives and your fortunes. Are you willing that this hellish conspiracy shall be permitted to go on undisturbed until the wicked traitors who are engaged in it shall have accomplished their designs, until you are bound hand and foot, and chained to the car of despotism by fetters that cannot be broken; or will you at once awake to a realization of the impending danger, and by a united effort strangle the monster?

For the purpose of exposing to the world the secret means by which this treasonable order has been so far successful in the accomplishment of its great end the dismemberment of our Republic, this publication is made. We have no wish, or design, to cause unnecessary alarm, or to arouse the passions; but our leading object is to convince the loyal people of the United States that their liberties are at this moment in greater danger from the secret enemies in their own midst and the foreign enemies of our institutions who are in league with them, than from the armed hordes who are now in rebellion against the government.

The secrets of the K. G. C. are very carefully guarded, and we are not yet able to reveal to the world all that we could wish; but the work of investigation is in competent and faithful hands, and we hope that we shall be able hereafter to make known all the secret means by which this vile conspiracy is carried on.

The following exposition of the work of the K. G. C., was first published in the columns of the *Louisville Journal*, in July, 1861. Of its authenticity there can be no doubt. Geo. D. Prentice, Esq., the editor of the *Journal*, gives his "solemn assurance as an editor and as a man," that the documents from which he derived his information are authentic. He asserts, moreover, that he received them from a prominent Knight of the Third Degree. The genuineness of these documents has never yet been denied by any man whose word can be regarded as valid testimony in the case. Corroborative evidence was furnished in a violent newspaper quarrel, which occurred soon after the first publication was made, in which several "Knights of the Third Degree" in the city of Louisville were participants, the question in dispute being as to the authorship of the revelations made to Mr. PRENTICE. After the warfare had subsided, he informed them that they were all mistaken, and that each one of the parties implicated was equally guiltless.

That the work, in many of its details, has been essentially changed since the first publication of this exposition, we are well aware. But enough remains to convince the loyal people of the United States that the objects and plans of the K. G. C. are inimical to the best interests of the country, and that this diabolical organization should be exposed in all its enormity, and crushed by the strong arm of power. Since its introduction into the North Western States and Canada, the order has adopted a *modus operandi* materially differing from that herein revealed, and perhaps better suited to its new field of operations. Its most active members are among the noisiest of the pretended friends of the Union; and there is reason to suspect that it has its emissaries in high and confidential positions in the civil and military departments of our government. Its real designs are cloaked under a specious garb of patriotism, and of intense solicitude for the preservation of the Union, and for the welfare of our people. The revelations here made should convince the most incredulous that the true objects of the members of this order are of the basest sort; and that they are utterly unscrupulous as to the means by which their ends are to be attained. They are banded together by the most solemn obligations, to obey the orders of their commanders, whatever they may be; and it is evident that human life is held to be of but little value, should it offer an obstacle to the accomplishment of the objects sought.

We now proceed to give the details of the work, together with such remarks of the editor of the *Louisville Journal* as are of permanent and general application:

From the Louisville Journal, July 18, 1861.

We are not prepared to state how long the Order of the Knights of the Golden Circle has been in existence. It never assumed in public estimation much importance until after the springing up of the great question of Union or Disunion in our land. It is believed to have materially changed its character since then, and certainly it has played a prominent part in the political affairs of the nation. It is an intensely Disunion concern. Its members bear the same relation to other Disunionists that regular soldiers do to the militia. The association is upheld and applauded as patriotic and noble by the whole Disunion press everywhere. Every imputation made against it is resented by the Disunion press as a blow at the Disunion cause.

The success with which the Knights of the Golden Circle have kept the secrets of their Order has been a matter of wonder to many. The Chief of the Order has pretended to publish all the written portion of the Ritual or Rituals, but we know perfectly well that he was attempting a fraud upon the community. Hundreds of members of the Order have sworn dreadful oaths that they would kill any one of their fellows who should dare to reveal, and any editor or printer who should be guilty of publishing their mysteries. Probably the knowledge of these oaths has kept many persons silent who felt that they were under a solemn obligation to their fellow men to speak what they knew. For ourselves, we care not for their threats. A public man is miserably unfit for his station, if he hesitates to do his duty, and trust the consequences to God and his fellow men.

We have before us all the secret documents of the Order of the Knights of the Golden Circle. That they are authentic, we give our solemn assurance as an editor and as a man. We proceed to publish such portions as will give a correct and full idea of the character and purposes and plans of the Order.

There are three Degrees to the Order; the first Military, the second Financial, the third Governmental.

The Ritual of the First Degree contains little of special importance. We will here premise that the reading of the Rituals is entirely unintelligible except by the aid of keys, a great many numerical figures being substituted for words. We are in possession of the keys, and, in what we publish of the Rituals, we shall give it just as we find it, putting into parenthesis the meaning of the figures. The two following paragraphs are from the Obligation taken in the First Degree, the words of the first being spoken by the Treasurer, and those of the second by an officer called the Captain:

Treasurer. Gentlemen, we must now tell you that the first field of our operations is 2 (Mexico); but we hold it to be our duty to offer our services to any Southern State to repel a Northern army. We hope such a contingency may not occur. But whether the Union is reconstructed or not, the Southern States must foster any scheme having for its object the Americanization and Southernization of 2 (Mexico), so that in either case our success will be certain.

Captain. Under the laws of 2 (Mexico) every emigrant receives from the State authorities a grant of 640 acres of land. Under a treaty closed with 3 (Manual Doblado, Governor of Guanajuato) on the 11th of February, 1860, we are invited to Colonize in 2 (Mexico) to enable the best people there to establish a permanent government. We agree to introduce a force of 16,000 men, armed, equipped, and provided, and to take the field under the command of 3 (Manual Doblado, Governor of Guanajuato), who agrees to furnish an equal number of men to be officered by K. G. C.'s. To cover the original expenses of arming our forces, there is mortgaged to our Trustees the right to collect one half the annual revenues of 4 (Guanajuato) until we are paid the sum of $840,000. As a bonus there is also ceded to us 355,000 acres of land. The pay of the army is the same as the regular army of 2 (Mexico), which is about one eighth more than that of the United States. To secure this there is mortgaged to us all the public property of 4 (Guanajuato), amounting in taxable value to $23,000,000. 3 (Manual Doblado, Governor of Guanajuato) is now there, making arrangements for our reception. We shall cross over as soon as possible after our own national troubles are settled.

We presume that Mexico will feel herself under obligations to us for this exposition of the designs entertained towards her by the Knights of the Golden Circle and their Mexican accomplice, the Governor of Guanajuato. We will now add the following from the Ritual of the first Degree:

Captain—I will now give you the signs, grips, password, and token of the First Degree of the K. C. G. (Of course a misprint for K. G. C.) This Degree has a name, which I may now give you—it is the "1," (Knight of the Iron Hand.) The first great sign of the Order is thus made, 7 (hands open, palms touching and resting on the top of the head; fingers pointed upwards). The answer to this is 8 (open hands touching shoulder where epaulettes are worn; elbows close to the side). These are battle field signs, and are not to be used under ordinary circumstances. The common sign of recognition is 9 (right fore finger drawn across upper lip under nose, as if rubbing). The answer 10 (with fore finger and thumb of left hand take hold of left ear). To gain admission to a Working Castle, or the room of any K. G. C., give 11 (one distinct rap) at the door. The Sentinel on duty will then raise the wicket and demand the countersign, which is 12 (SOLDIERS, always lettered except at Castle door). You will then pass to the center of the room and give the true sign of the K. G. C.; it is 13 (left hand on heart; right hand raised). This will be recognized by a bow from the Captain, when you will at once take your seat. The sign of assent is 14 (both hands up); of dissent 15 (one hand up); the grip is 16 (press with thumb one inch above second knuckle); the token 17 (Golden Circle enclosing block hands closed on scroll; the whole to be the size of a dime). Every member may wear the sign of his degree.

And now, reader, you know as much about the signs, grips, tokens, &c., of the Knights of the Golden Circle as they themselves do. We may here remark that the initiation fee for the First Degree is one dollar, for the Second five dollars, for the Third ten.

From the Second or Financial Degree, we need give but little. The following is the closing part of the initiation:

Captain. The headquarters of this Organization are at 23 (Monterey); where most of the stores and munitions are deposited. The Financial Headquarters are at ——; Col. N. J. Scott is at present Financial Chairman. * * *

Inspector. * * *

Lieutenant. * * *

Captain. I shall now give you the unwritten parts of this work, and I trust you will be careful in its use. If a general war ensues, we shall dispense with the First Degree and rely on this and the Third.

Name—18 (True Faith:) sign—25 (fore finger and thumb of right hands joined, while with the rest of the hand upon the right eye is touching with middle finger,) answer—26 (same with left hand and left eye); password 27 (Monterey); night word of distress—32 (St. Mary); response—31 and say 5 (grasp by wrist and say Rio Grande); emblem—28 (gold circle encasing Greek cross in center of which is star.) This is the 29 (key) to our 30 (secret alphabet); use of 33 (K. G. C.) 56 (George Bickley); guard sign ½ 28 (gold circle encasing Greek cross in center of which is a star); silence 25 (fore finger and thumb of right hand joined, while with the rest of the hand open the right eye is touching with middle finger) on hips; danger—right—same with left.

And now it remains for us to give the Ritual of the Third Degree, which, as being the most important, we shall publish almost entire. We have not the time or space for commenting on it now. Every citizen can judge of it for himself. The Roman Catholics and the foreign-born population will see how they are proscribed by this mysterious Order—this central and guiding power of the Secession and Disunion party. All will see, too, that the Order declare for a Monarchy, a Limited Monarchy as they call it, until all their purposes in regard to Mexico shall have been accomplished; and we need not suggest how brief will be the period within which, if they get their *Limited* Monarchy, they will make it an *Absolute* Monarchy.

THIRD OR POLITICAL DEGREE OF THE 33 (K. G. C.)—NAMED 57 (Knights of the Columbian Star).

INSTRUCTIONS: Officers of the Council shall be a Governor and a Secretary. Every 57 (Knight of the Columbian Star) is qualified to act in either capacity.

Qualifications for Membership.

Candidates must be familiar with the work of the two former Degrees; must have been born in 58 (a Slave State), or if in 59 (a Free State) he must be a citizen; 60 (a Protestant) and 61 (a Slaveholder). A candidate who was born in 58 (a Slave State) need not be 61 (a Slaveholder) provided he can give 62 (Evidence of character as a Southern man).

Object: To form a Council for the 33 (K. G. C.) and to organize 63 (a Government) for 2 (Mexico). No 57 (Knight of the Columbian Star) shall admit, except to a brother 57, that he has this Degree, for reasons that will hereafter appear. Any two 57's can confer the Degree on others, the oldest 57 acting as Governor.

Council Hall. * * *

Approaching Candidates.—Of course all 33 (K. G. C.) know each other. There being two 57 in hailing distance of the court house of said county—that is, 64 (within the county). They will confer together as to the worthiness of any 33, whom they may think a proper person to be made a 57, and, having agreed, one or both of them will go to the person, each knowing the other is a 33, and tell him that there is a gentleman 64 (within the county) who has the power to confer the Third Degree, and propose to him that all three shall, or more, if so the case is, go and apply for it—telling him, or them, at the same time, that the fee will be 65 (ten dollars.) If he assents, propose a time and place, and all be punctual. Let it not be exactly the place where the Degree is to be conferred, but near. The 57 (Knights of the Columbian Star) act as if *they* also sought the Degree. Also, tell the candidate that, as he or you may be rejected, it will be expected that he will not mention the matter to any one till the result is known.

When in the room, the Governor will take the Bible, and will cause all to lay their hands thereon, when each will repeat after the Governor the following.

INITIATION.

We three, (or other number, as the case may be) citizens of 58, (a Slave State) do hereby and herein, in the presence of each other and the Great Jehovah, solemnly and sincerely pledge our faith and honor to conceal and never reveal to any mortal being, save such as we know to be 57, (Knights of the Columbian Star) any circumstance or thing that may here transpire during the next hour, and to keep the knowledge of this hour forever secret from all but 57. In the name of God. Amen!

[All take seats.]

Secretary—What are you that you are thus leading off in this work, with which you seem so familiar?

GOVERNOR—I am, what you are, a 57; you being the Secretary and I the Governor of this Council, and I here promise to conscientiously do my duty at all times while I hold fellowship with the 33. But, sir, will you explain why it was necessary to proceed as we have?

SECRETARY—We thus proceeded because the laws of the Order demand it—and because the Order will lose its efficiency as soon as it ceases to be absolutely secret. It is not permitted that we shall be known to any person living except to those who are 57. You will find nothing in the Order of which to be ashamed. Not even the 33 must know who has this Degree. This is, perhaps, the only real secret order in the world. *It must be kept secret!*

GOVERNOR: [To Candidate] I have a few questions to ask you, which I trust you will answer without reserve, for I pledge you my word as a man, as a 57, and as Governor of this Council, that I am in earnest in this work, and would not have sought you out, unless I had thought this whole work would meet your unqualified approbation.

1. Give me the sign, password and grip of a 1 (Knight of the Iron Hand.)
2. Give me the signs, password, and grip of a 18 (True Faith).
3. To what 66 (Castle) do you belong?
4. Where were you born?
5. Where was your father and mother born?
6. Are you 60 (a Protestant) or 67 (a Roman Catholic)?
7. Where do you now live?
8. Do you belong to any other secret society?
9. Married or single?
10. Are you 61 (a Slaveholder)?
11. Will you stand firm in your obligation of the 33 (K. G. C.)?
12. Do you believe in the religion of Jesus Christ?
13. Are you willing to help in spreading it?

SECRETARY: Judging from what you have seen of the 33 project, and by what you know of us, are you now willing to be united with us in a society from which you can never resign, but which can in no way compromise you, since the only work and responsibilities we put on you are these:

1. Secrecy as to who the 57 are.
2. To attend every call of a Council made by the Governor General of this State.
3. To do for every brother what every brother has sworn to do for you.
4. To inform the nearest working brother known to you, of danger to the 33 or 57.
5. To exercise a cautious prudence in counteracting false impressions of the 33, and to report to 56 (George Bickley) or his successor or successors any improper or dangerous actions you may know of.
6. To respond to the call of any brother in your county.
7. And never to speak of the work and character of this Degree of the 33 to any one except 57 only as you express sentiments taught by the Order.

We shall not force you to work unless you desire to do so—but on the call of five brothers you must respond, if in your power so to do. Once a 57 (Knight of the Columbian Star) so you will live and die, though no mortal man may know it but 57.

GOVERNOR: Are you willing to proceed?
(Candidate answers, Yes.)
SECRETARY: Every knee shall bend to God, and every tongue confess his name.
GOVERNOR: Brothers, we will kneel for prayer. * * *
GOVERNOR: Mr. Secretary, collect the fees of this (or these) candidates, and we will proceed in the work of initiation.

OBLIGATION DELIVERED BY GOVERNOR.

Before God and these witnesses, I do vow that I will never reveal the signs, grips, passwords, tokens or significants of the 57 (Knights of the Columbian Star) to any man, woman or child, except to a 57 in good and lawful standing, and then only as hereafter directed, and for the lawful purposes of this Order. And I pledge and commit myself fully and freely to each of the following obligations, and in perfect good faith:

1st. I vow and promise to conceal the names of the 57, the objects and character thereof, and never to speak of the same as though I was a member, except to those who can give me our sacred word in such a way as to satisfy me they are 57.

2d. No matter what secrets may be given to me by a 57, if given as the secret of a 57 and because I am one, I will hold the same sacredly in my own knowledge, and never recommunicate it even to a 57 (Knight of the Columbian Star), unless authorized so to do by the brother whose secret it is. I will never speak evil of a brother 57, either before his face or behind his back. I will never dishonor the wife or daughter of a 57, I knowing them to be such, but I will shield and protect the character of all 57 whom I may know to be such—their wives, daughters, and families.

3d. I will oppose to the utmost of my ability, and never consent, but vote against the admission of any confirmed drunkard, professional gambler, rowdy, convict, felon, 68 (Abolitionist), negro, Indian, minor, idiot or 69 (Foreigner), to membership in this department of the 33. But I will get as many good and eligible 70 (Southern born men) to join this Degree as I can.

4th. * * *
5th. * * *

6th. I do promise and vow that I will use my best exertions to find out any and every 68 (Abolitionist) in my county, whether 71 (man, woman, or child), and forward the name of such to 56 (George Bickley), or his lawful successor, or in case I remain in the 72 (United States) after 56 and the 33 have gone to the 2 (Mexico), I will report the same to the Governor General of this State, and I will keep a close watch on all such, and report at every meeting of my Council, for the information of the 57 remaining in the 72 (United States). If I know of any 68 who is a 73 (stranger or traveler) trading with 100 (negroes), or doing any other unlawful act, I will at once inform all 57 in my county—whereupon the *Captain* of the county shall call the 57 to meet in Council, that proper steps may be taken for 74 (his exposure).

7th. If any 75 (insurrection) shall be started, and it comes to my knowledge, I will do all I have promised above. Or should my State, or any other 76 (Southern State) be 77 (invaded) by 68 (Abolitionists) I will muster the largest force I can and go to the scene of danger, if well and able to go. I further promise to do all I can to build up a public sentiment in my State favorable to 18, (the expulsion of free negroes) that they may be sent to 2 (Mexico). I further promise that no 79 (free negro) shall marry 80 (my slave), or 80 marry a 79 if I can prevent it.

8th. I also promise to report to the Governor-General of the State the names of all 67 (Roman Catholic) ministers in my county as well as of all 31 (Northern Teachers), and no 69 (Foreigner) or 68 (Abolitionist) shall ever receive this degree if I can prevent it—one negative vote only being necessary to reject any one from receiving this degree, which vote must be taken before the candidate has been approached.

9th. I will protect and defend all widows and orphans to the best of my ability, and especially those of a 57. And I vow I will never desert the 57 or their cause and aims while three members remain and consent to propagate it. And should they succeed in 82 (conquering and Southernizing) the whole or any part of 2 (Mexico), I will do all I can to prevent any 67 (Roman Catholic) from being appointed to any office of profit or trust, and even in the 72 (U. S.) I will always give the preference to 60 (a Protestant), and especially to 57. I will do all I can as an honorable man, to make 58 (a Slave State) of 2. As such, I will urge its 83 (Annexation) to 72 (U. S.), otherwise I will oppose it with equal zeal. In 2 I will endeavor to cause to be opened to the public all 84 (Nunneries, Monasteries, or Convents), and there shall be no advantages to 67 (Roman Catholic) which is not equally accorded to 60 (Protestant). The 60 [Bible] shall be adopted for use in all public schools, and any 85 [Priest] who shall be detected in 86 [Gambling or violating the ordinance of religion] shall be expelled from 2. Any minister holding any place under the Government must be 60 [Protestant].

10th. All civil places of prominence shall be given, as far as my influence goes, to 57 (Knights of the Columbian Star), and when these are supplied to the 18 (True Faith); then to the 1 (Knights of the Iron Hand). I will advocate the establishment of 63 (A Government), which shall place the power in the hands of the most educated and moral, and oppose the recognition of any 87 (Negro, Mulatto, Indian, or mixed blood) to citizenship. I will sustain the effort to reduce the 88 (Peon System) to 89 (Perpetual Slavery), and to divide them to 1 (Knights of the Iron Hand,) 18 (True Faith), and 57 (Knights of the Columbian Star), in proportion of 1, 2, 3, to have and hold forever. But the same laws shall be enacted for their protection as are recognized in every other 58 (Slave State).

11th. Until the whole civil, political, financial and religious reconstruction of 2 (Mexico) has been completed, I will recognize 90 (Limited Monarchy) as the best form of 63 (Government) for the purpose in view, since it can be made strong and effective.

12th. To prevent the entrance of any 68 (Abolitionist) into 2 (Mexico), I will sustain a passport system, and any and every 73 (stranger or traveler) shall go before the customs officer at the port of his entry, and there take an oath, stating whether he intends to become a citizen, and if so, that he will sustain and support the Government then in existence, and that he will not interfere with the system of 89 (perpetual slavery) then recognized, but that he will obey the laws then recognized. If he be a traveler merely, he shall give up his passport to the Chief of Police on his entrance into each town, and which shall be returned to him on demand of the same officer, when about to leave for another place. And any 73 who shall pass or attempt to pass without a passport, shall be arrested and expelled from the country, and upon resistance he shall be shot, but every traveler so entering 2 (Mexico) must be informed of this rule.

13th. The successor to 56 (Geo. Bickley) must be over thirty years of age, of Southern birth, liberally educated, a 57 (Knight of the Columbian Star) sound of body and mind and married and 60 (a protestant). He shall swear to carry out this policy and to extend 91 (slavery) over the whole of 92 (Central America) if in his power. He shall try to acquire 93 (Cuba) and control 94 (the Gulf of Mexico). No one else will I sustain. But for such a one, who must be proposed by 95 (Cabinet Minister) and elected by all 57 or a majority of them, I will sustain here, there, or elsewhere. When the 33 (K. G. C.) cross the 5 (Rio Grande) I will do all I can to send in 96 (recruits for the army), and if ever I should cease to be an active worker for the 57, I will keep secret what I know of the real character of the organization, and I promise never to confer this degree in any other way than in the way I have received it, and I will forward to 56 (Geo. Bickley) or the Governor-General of this State the names and fees of every candidate whom I shall initiate as Governor. In witness, I do voluntarily, here in these presence, sign my name and P. O. address. (Governor asks, "Will you sign?")

SECRETARY.—Perhaps you had better hear the whole degree and then sign, for unless we have your entire approbation, we do not wish to commit you to anything. I am well aware that this whole scheme is a bold and daring one, that can but surprise you at first, as it did me, and for this reason I beg to state a few facts for your consideration. In the rise and progress of Democracy in America we have seen its highest attainment. In the very outset it was based on high religious principles, and adopted as a refuge from despotism. In the North, Puritanism molded it, and went so far as to leave out the natural conservative element of all Democracies—97 (domestic slavery.) As a result, we have presented now social, religious and political anarchy. From Millerism and Spiritualism, every Utopian idea has numerous advocates. The manufacturer is an aristocrat, while the working man is a serf. The latter class, constantly goaded by poverty, seek a change—they care not what it may be. Democracy unrestrained by 97 (domestic slavery) multiplies the manufacturing classes indefinitely—but it debases the mechanic. Who ever knew a practical shoemaker or a maker of pinheads to have a man's ambition? They own neither land or property, and have no tie to the institutions of the country. The Irishman emigrates, and the Frenchman stays at home. The one hates his country—the other adores his. The Frenchman is a slaveholder and a man. The Irishman is a serf and an outcast. The South is naturally agricultural, and the farmer being most of the time in the midst of his growing crops, seeing the open operation of nature, his mind expands, he grows proud and ambitious of all around, and feels himself a man. He wants no change either in civil, religious or political affairs. He cultivates the soil, and it yields him the means to purchase labor. He becomes attached to home and its associations, and remains forever a restrained Democrat—restrained by moral and civil laws from any and all overt acts. He needs and makes a centralized government, because his property is at stake when anarchy prevails.

GOVERNOR: Now in the case of 2 [Mexico] suppose we were to elevate to citizenship 87 [Negro, Mulatto, Indian, or mixed blood], do you not see at once that the very act would undo all the results of 82 [Conquering and Southernizing]? We should be voted back to 72 [U. S.] the day of the first election. None but white 89 [land-holders] should be allowed the exercise of the citizen's franchise. These are the men who pay the taxes and guard the people. Again, efficient officers require experience which can only be acquired by time—hence places should be held as long as the holder can discharge faithfully and efficiently his functions.

SECRETARY: You will therefore see that we labor not only for the extension of 97 [Domestic Slavery] in 2, but that we seek to make 63 [a Government] strong enough to protect and perpetuate it. The means for erecting a 90 [Limited Monarchy] are in 2. They only require to be used well. We require a vast number of officers—some thousands in all. Now help us make 63 [a Government] and go you and send your son and let him take his place. The work is large, and there are plenty of us to do it. Of course the whole scheme must be managed well. As soon as everything is reduced to order, then we may canvass the question of a Republic.

GOVERNOR: Vast sums will be needed. 2 can furnish every dollar. The day we cross 5 [Rio Grande] parties in 99 [Matamoras] will advance us $1,000,000, and others at 23 [Monterey] $2,000,000. The revenue of those two places amounts to $7,000,000, and the other cities in 24 [Northern Mexico] very large sums. The 33 then is only a repetition of the East India Co., or the Hudson Bay Co. You are now a stockholder. Help us to get in the field with your money and your influence—help us to procure material, for you are as much interested as any of us. Money will follow our success. We shall concentrate in 20 [Encinal Co., Texas], by Sept. 15th, 1860, [a misprint, we presume, for 1861—ED. JOURNAL], and we will cross 5 [Rio Grande] by the 1st day of 6 [October]. Now, Sir, if you will be one of us, either to go or to stay at home, you will sign your name as all of us have done, after which I will give you the Ceremonial of this Degree. [*Candidates sign at the end of the work; and he also signs his own work.*].

SECRETARY: The signs, test-signs, words and pass-words, grips and pass-grips, tokens and keys of this degree must be well learned, for on their proper use depends your standing in this order. Notice them, practice them, and heed them.

[The candidate is here made to sign the obligation, as also a copy for himself. When he has done this, present him with a copy and a key of the degree.]

SIGNS, &c.—(These are now to be given in full, and explained.) ☞ See Key.

The key form mentioned we have. We will give it in such form that the reader will understand it. The sign is *a* (raise hat with left hand over right, open hand on top of head.) The countersign is *b* (left hand with hat extended to right angles, hand by side.) The silent sign is *c* (left hand on back of head.) The answer is *d* (right hand on forehead, then extended.) The night sign is *e* (two distinct claps of hands, and repeat once.) The test sign is *f* (finger and thumb of left hand take hold of lip.) The sacred word is *g* (Eloi.) The password is *h* (Andalusia), and to this is added in parenthesis, "Notice instructions in use of words." The night word given with *e* is *i* (high.) The grip is *j* (as given.) The pass grip is *k* (same with left hand still holding by right.) The token or emblem is *l* (same as shown.) The answer to *f* is *m* (right thumb and fore finger on pit of stomach.)

The following is the secret alphabet of the K. G. C. It is to be written on ruled paper, the rule line forming the base, whence the various characters radiate:

A B C D E F G H I J K L M N

O P Q R S T U V W X Y Z & .

That's all we have at present to give, and, as we have said, it may be relied on as authentic. It is a revelation of the mysteries of an Order which claims to be, and no doubt is, powerful in our land. Its emissaries have lured into it thousands of young men, by impressing them with utterly false ideas of its nature and designs. The members of the First and Second Degrees know nothing of the Third, although they are unwittingly guided and controlled by it. Let them examine the revolting character of the obligations of the Third Degree, and then make all haste to repudiate an organization that deserves the scorn and abhorrence of all just men.

The Roman Catholics and foreign-born citizens will find much in the Ritual of the Third Degree deserving their attention. Irishmen, in particular, will meet with something interesting to themselves.

The K. G. C.'s of the Third Degree, it seems, look keenly to office. They require that *all* of the members of their Degree shall have offices before any member of the Second Degree can be accommodated, and that *all* the members of the Second Degree shall be provided with offices before a solitary individual of the First can be accommodated. But then they say that they are going to have thousands of offices, and they mean that the incumbents of offices shall hold on for life.

It is no wonder that the members of the Third Degree, Knights of the Columbian Star, as they call themselves, guard carefully in their Ritual against ever being known as such, even to their brethren of the First and Second Degrees.

Let all bear steadily in mind that the Order of Knights of the Golden Circle is now and has all along been the central sun of the Secession party of Kentucky

In a subsequent issue of the *Louisville Journal*, the editor says :

We have every reason to believe that the blow which we dealt to the Order of the Knights of the Golden Circle in publishing their rituals, signs, passwords, &c., was a death-blow. The Order may linger on for a time, but the remnant of its existence is destined to be miserably sickly and very brief. Our exposition has been published everywhere, except in the South, the papers in that section not having the virtue or the courage to aid in revealing the character of an Order devoted to Disunion, no matter how shameful and wicked its principles may be.

Three or four of the Secession newspapers, evidently grateful to the Knights of the Golden Circle for their active and important political aid, have spoken of our exposition as "bogus." None of them, audacious as they are, have ventured to assert directly that our exposition was not genuine and strictly correct, for they know that it was, and they furthermore know that they could not assert the contrary without causing themselves to be regarded by the universal public as unscrupulous falsifiers. If we deemed it at all necessary for the accomplishment of an important purpose to prove the genuineness and truth of what we published, we could readily do so, but it is not necessary, for no one has or can have an honest doubt upon the subject. How we obtained the secrets of the Order we shall never state; it is enough to say, that we received them in such a way that we had a right to give them to the world.

The whole number of persons that have been admitted into the Order in this city is nearly or quite three thousand, but by far the greater part of them were from other places, and a good many have gone as adventurers to the Southern Confederacy. The number of members of the First and Second Degrees now in this city is perhaps four or five hundred. Not a few of them are honest and well-meaning young men who have been seduced into the Order by selfish and cunning electioneerers, the object being to obtain their money and their votes, and, if necessary, the strength of their right arms, they being all the while controlled by a secret power above them, a power working in darkness and mystery. If, however, the members of the First and Second Degrees continue after this their connection with the accursed Order, the excuse of ignorance and innocence cannot be pleaded in their behalf.

Of course the members of the Order, now that their secrets are known, may get up new signs and signals and words, and undoubtedly they will do so, if they think it worth their while to try to keep their Order alive. Already we have heard of one change. The password, by which a member gained admission to the meetings, was "Soldiers," and this, since our exposition, has been changed to "Davis Soldiers." At the next meeting it will have to be changed to something else.

Of this exposition, and of the arch-traitor who is the ostensible head of the order of the K. G. C., a writer in *The World* thus says:

"The recent disclosures of the *Louisville Journal* of the mysteries of the secrets of the society of the Knights of the Golden Circle, have not met the consideration they deserve. It would be enough to laugh at the K. G. C., if General George Washington Bickley, who pretends to be the President of the Society, were really its master. The General, it is said, is one less likely to bleed his enemies than his friends. Great is his strategy in campaigns of peculation, and wonderful his bravery in attacking the well-defended purses of his friends. Tremble when the General approaches, if you have a dollar unprotected by a cannon. Yet, though he is terrible as an army making war upon your pocket, he is as harmless as a lamb in any other capacity. So far as *he* is concerned, we have no fears of the K. G. C., but, on the contrary, confess to a sincere pity for its members. But Gen. G. W. Bickley is a mere tool. The K. G. C. is under the control of men, each of whom is to *him* more than Iago to Roderigo. Gen. B., in 1860, induced a gentleman of respectability, then residing in Kentucky, to cash a check for a few hundred dollars on a bank in which he had no funds. The General had previously given to this gentleman documents of great interest, which are now in our possession, and throw new light on the disclosures in the *Journal*. They are of greater service still—they show the secret relations of the K. G. C. to the present rebellion, and its connection with the Confederate Government."

Among the documents referred to in the above extract, is an address of the Convention of the K. G. C., held at Raleigh, N. C., on the 7th of May. 1860, to the people of the Southern States. In this pamphlet the purposes of the K. G. C. are declared in language the most emphatic. It declares the K. G. C. to have been organized in 1854, *as a military organization*, intended to make the South independent of the North, either in or out of the Union. Its great object is the establishment of a colony in Mexico, and the possession of Mexico *by the South* is declared to be an absolute necessity of political equality, *in the Union or out of it*. It contains an eloquent description of the fruitfulness of Mexico; of her Flora and Pomona; of the wondrous fertility of her soil, and its undeveloped capacity for the production of cotton, sugar and tobacco; of her six thousand miles of sea coast; of her rich mines of gold and silver; of the suitability of her climate to slave labor; and last, but by no means least, of the enormous wealth of the Romish Church in Mexico, and the advantages of the *confiscation of three hundred millions of dollars to the use of the K. G. C.!* The military force of the order is stated to be 16,000, and it is claimed that 100,000 men could be mustered if the money could be obtained to put them in the field. The entire membership in 1860 is given at 48,000. From the statements in this address, the following facts are made plain:

1. That the K. G. C. has been for seven years arming the South against fancied oppression by the North.
2. That it has always declared itself independent of the North.
3. That it denies the existence of any responsible government in Mexico, and would usurp full power over the people.
4. That it would impose slavery upon Mexico as a permanent institution, *and would re-open the slave trade.*
5. That it has always been on the best terms with the Southern State governments, and that *its policy is identical with that of secession.*

All these plans in regard to Mexico have been temporarily postponed, but not abandoned. The address says, "that the Southern Governors will have use for us in the next six months is confidently expected. If so, the K. G. C. may find its *Mexico in the District of Columbia!*"

That the K. G. C. planned the assassination of Mr. LINCOLN, either on his journey to the Capitol, or during the ceremonies of his inauguration, scarcely admits of a doubt. The plot was discovered and revealed to his friends long before his departure from his home for the city of Washington, and was frustrated by the vigilance of his friends and the military precaution of GEN. SCOTT.

Enough has been revealed in regard to this wicked and treacherous organization to convince every man of sane mind that it is dangerous in the extreme; that it seeks the overthrow of our government, the disruption of the great American Union; the seizure, by fraud or by force, of the territory of our southern neighbors, with whom we are at peace, and the acquisition of an immense extent of territory in which slavery shall be made the leading institution, from which the free white laboring man shall be excluded, or in which he shall be reduced to the condition of a serf, and where a Paradise may be established for the exclusive benefit of the effete and bloated aristocracy of South Carolina, and the few despotic masters of the reckless cut-throats and ruffians who compose the rank and file of the K. G. C.

But our task is not yet done. We propose now to give some evidence of the existence and thorough organization of this order among our neighbors of Canada, and among the nobility, aristocracy and moneyed classes in England.

From the first outbreak of the present rebellion, the tone of the British Press towards the Government and people of the loyal portion of the United States, has been of the most hostile and ungracious character; and a careful comparison of the articles which have appeared in a majority of the leading British newspapers, with those published in the South, shows unmistakable evidence of identity of origin. All have been dictated in the same spirit, and, probably, to a great extent, by the same parties. In the discussions arising out of the arrest of SLIDELL and MASON, the similarity of tone and temper was too palpable to be overlooked. The British Press teemed with unfounded slanders upon our Government and people. The public mind of England was inflamed by the publication of deliberate falsehoods, wholesale vituperation, and the foulest calumnies, such as could originate nowhere else than in the distempered brains of men who viewed every thing from the secession stand-point, and who were determined to accomplish, so far as was in their power, the disruption of the Union by means of a foreign war, and the establishment of two separate confederacies within its limits. That a large and powerful interest in England was determined on war with the United States, was perfectly plain. Whence came these indisputable manifestations of bitter hostility towards the United States, in consequence of an affair which every sensible man in England knew could and would be amicably arranged, and adjusted without a resort to arms? Whence came the palpable and wicked falsehoods which were used to inflame the public mind against the only true friends that England ever had upon the face of the globe? Whence came all the insult and the vituperation against us, which disgraced the British Press and the British people in the eyes of the civilized world—whence but from the K. G. C. and its allies abroad?

The following letter is from the pen of a gentleman who has had ample opportunity to make himself acquainted with the facts whereof he writes, and who has devoted much time to the investigation of the secret and treacherous designs which he reveals. His language shows him to be an intelligent man. The statement which he makes is corroborated by proof which is within the reach of every man who is conversant with the tone of the British and Southern Press, and who closely watches events as they transpire. This statement should be accepted as proof positive of the truth of the revelations made, unless disproved by evidence of the most convincing character. Neither the word nor the oath of any member or of any number of members of the K. G. C. will suffice to refute this evidence of the treasonable character of the conspiracy in which they are engaged:

DEAR SIR,—Your note has been received, asking for such information as I may have of the objects and working of the secret conclave of traitors in the Northern States, known as the "Knights of the Golden Circle" (K. G. C). I have devoted considerable time and attention to this organization, and my opportunities have been very rare for gaining information. And here let me say, it is the sworn duty of every K. G. C., who is true to his obligation, to deny the existence of the organization, not generally by *positive* denials, but by heaping ridicule on the *idea* of such an organization, which implies that all Northern men are not loyal. There is, however, *ample and positive proof* that the Order of K. G. C. is thoroughly organized in *every Northern State*, as auxiliary to the Southern rebellion. It assumes various shapes and colors, yet all working under the same system of operations, and all aiming at the same end. The designation of "K. G. C." having become unpopular on account of the known treasonable designs of that Order, it is protean in its character, and sails under different cognomens to best effect its purpose—sometimes being the "Peace Party," the "Union Party," the "Constitutional Party," the "Democratie Society," "Club," or "Association," the "Mutual Protection;" and, since the

"*Indiana leak,*" as they call it, about the "M. P.'s," they have chosen "S. P.," or "Self Protection," as a name. And since you ask for facts only, I may say it is properly a secret *political* treason party, as its members *initiated* are all most strictly limited to the known members of one political party.

THE IMMEDIATE OBJECT is the overthrow of the Government established by our patriot sires, baptized in their life-blood, and handed down to us, to be forever defended and protected, as the best form of government ever given to man. THE ULTIMATE OBJECT, *the spoils of Office and the control of the Government,* by the party which sustains the efforts of these "knights" of treason. The great majority of the most active *leaders* are those who have heretofore enjoyed the emoluments of place in the government, and wish to be restored to power. For this purpose they are willing to tear down the old fabric and erect a new one upon its ruins. They have some definite plans of operation, forming a strong net-work of treason around the Union, well calculated to draw in many true men to be used by them unawares in carrying out their plots. I will refer briefly to a few of the means they use.

1. THEY WISH TO PROLONG THE WAR, hoping that something may turn up to get their Southern rebel friends out of their position, without being made to acknowledge the supremacy of the Constitution and the Union. They hope and work for a *foreign* war, to make that a pretext for stopping domestic strife, and uniting against a common foe. They are prolonging the war, also, for the purpose of tiring out the patience of the country, while they can make a public sentiment ready to "compromise" with armed rebellion—to do any thing honorable or dishonorable to stop the war. To do this, they appeal to the pockets of the people with exaggerated pictures of enormous *taxes,* and virtually say, that because it costs *money* to maintain the Union, we ought to surrender at discretion to the demands of those who have taken up arms in rebellion against it.

2. THEY WORK BY TREACHERY.—Having first opposed the Government in asserting any authority to enforce the laws and maintain the Union and the Constitution, and done what they could to encourage the outbreak by tendering Northern sympathy and support in advance, they are now seeking to assist their friends in the Southern army, by getting themselves into positions to betray the Union cause for their benefit. In the month of August last, immediately after the disaster of Bull Run, they marked out a new programme, and sent messengers through all the loyal States to give their friends, the K. G. C., the *cue* for putting their new plan into extensive operation. The treachery of one of their men at the head of a column of the Federal army, who turned the tide of battle against us at Bull Run, worked so well, that they determined at once, during the re-organization of our army, to fill it with their own men for similar future operations. "Castles" were forthwith organized in all the States. Those who had been vomiting treason among their loyal neighbors, to the full extent that public sentiment would tolerate, now very suddenly and *mysteriously* become seemingly loyal and patriotic, and anxious for places to draw their swords in defense of the Union, and measure them with its rebellious foes. They wanted to be decorated with epaulettes. They would serve as Captains, and from that up to Colonels of Regiments, Brigadier and Major Generals. They wound a net-work of influences around Congress and the "powers that be," to retain men in the Departments, and to get others in—especially in the War Department—who were shining lights in the "Castles" of the K. G. C., for the avowed and *express purpose* of aiding the enemy, by treacherously watching, and conveying the secrets of the Government to the rebel army. Men were selected in the States, and sent hundreds of miles to Washington, with strong influences to back them, for this purpose. Better to carry out their project, they adroitly raised the "No-Party" cry, and by professing the most exalted and devoted loyalty, claimed the best places in which to betray the Union cause, for those who were trusted "Knights"—thus secretly plotting treason against the very cause that was to feed and clothe them! Among the K. G. C. of the Third Degree they freely calculate their prospects of success from the *treachery* of Federal officers, and especially of officers in the Union army, who, if occasion presents, are to disobey orders, and screen themselves behind flimsy excuses for allowing the enemy to escape, when, by acting in good faith, they might be defeated. They point to the singular escape of *Floyd* and his crew in Western Virginia, after Rosecrans had so decoyed them into a position that he was certain to bag the whole command, if orders had been faithfully executed by his subordinates. At the time of the Ball's Bluff disaster, they also gave knowing winks to indicate that it was the fulfilment of a chapter in their programme to disgust and dishearten the loyal North, discourage any advance movements, and encourage the rebel army with the report of victory. They claim a large number of the officers of Companies, Regiments, and Brigades, and Divisions, secretly to be in their interests, and even have the audacity to whisper that General MCCLELLAN understands their programme, and is not unfriendly to working up to it. They claim, also, a goodly number of friends and brethren in

the officers of the Navy. They deprecate the appointment of STANTON to the administration of the War Department, and regret that he is not one of their mystical number. They fear that all the influences they can throw around him will not induce him to bend his policy to favor their projects; yet they are ever on the alert, and will make a concerted effort, by pretended confidence and flattery, to weave an influence around him that will partially capture him, and control his policy. They acknowledge their faint hopes, however, of being able either to induce him to become a "Knight," or to lure him into their plausible scheme for the future control of the spoils of government.

3. PEACE CONVENTION AND NEW CONSTITUTION.—Another mode of arriving at their object, is a National Peace or Compromise Convention, to be held when all things are prepared. The schedule is to call a convention of all the States, North and South, to arrive at an understanding, and compromise the difficulties upon a basis already fixed. That basis is the Jeff. Davis Constitution of the Southern Confederacy—conceding and adopting some of its features, and yielding some of the important ones in our present instrument, as a "compromise." The main features of the compromise will be a constitutional recognition, guaranty, and protection of Slavery in the States and Territories, without distinction. In the mean time, the country being tired and sick of war and taxes, they expect to manufacture a public opinion that will adopt their scheme. To give popular strength to this "convention," there is to be a most earnest and persistent effort to carry every local and State election this year against the Administration, or War, and Union party—so that it will appear that the country has changed, and is against the further prosecution of the war for the supremacy of the old Union and the old Constitution *as it is;* and that the party calling the "National Peace Convention" are the majority or dominant party, and representing the public will. Further to facilitate party success at the polls, and cover up or draw attention from their own treasonable plottings against the Government, they are to join in a united and harmonious howl of "ABOLITIONIST" against all loyal men who sustain the Administration and the war to crush the rebellion; for the purpose of trying to identify and stigmatize them with the sins, and the long odious (in the North) doctrines and sentiments promulgated by a small band of fanatical disunionists, headed by Garrison and Wendell Phillips—claiming that all whom they may choose to call "Abolitionists," including the whole party that elected the Administration, and all who sustain it, in the prosecution of the war, are equally "traitors" with those who are in arms against the Union; and that, when the life of a Southern man, caught in the *overt act*, is sacrificed, the life of an "Abolitionist" should balance the account. While none but Southern men are in arms to overthrow the Government, the responsibility of the war is to be persistently charged upon the loyal North, which should be the first to offer terms of "peace" and "compromise." By throwing every obstacle in the way of the Government, added to secret treason, they hope to give plausibility, among the weak-minded, that whenever the control of the nation passes from their hands the country will get into trouble, and that the only party capable of governing the country is the one they lead—that peace and prosperity cannot return until *they* are restored to power. "Look at the country in a civil war in less than three months after the change of rulers," they say, with exulting triumph. No means are to be left untried to "divide and conquer" the war party at the polls. They have a systematic plan to discredit the Government in the eyes of the people. They cry aloud about frauds, while they are busily employed seeking contracts for the very purpose of defrauding the Government, to give coloring to their charges! If they cannot get original contracts, they seek sub-contracts from the friends of the Union, that the odium of their own dishonesty may fall on the shoulders of the War party. They boast of having already used these tactics to great effect. Doubting the ability of the Government to pay its liabilities, with a view of depreciating the public Securities and Treasury Notes, the withdrawal of public confidence, and cutting off the supplies to carry on the war, is another favorite scheme. It is seriously discussed in the "Castle" meetings, whether they will not utterly *refuse* to pay the war tax, which they think will not only embarrass the Government, but create a great public excitement that may demand the discontinuance of further resistance to the rebellion.

The demand for the exchange of prisoners, upon the terms dictated by Jeff. Davis, was an effort for the recognition of the "Confederacy," and to save the necks of the ring-leaders of the treason when they are eventually caught (as they expect they will be), by claiming to be "prisoners of war"—"belligerents"—instead of traitors to their Government. And when the war is over—whether the Union is re-established on its old basis, or upon the projected Jeff. Davis-Compromise-Constitution—the K. G. C. party are to assume all the credit of ending the conflict through their influence, and of having been the special friends of the rebels during their rebel lion, and thereby claim their political affinities and support in a consolidated party for the future control of the nation. They will divide and distract the Union party by a hypocritical support and flattery of the President and his policy, to create distrust in the minds of the real friends of the Administration, that it is not true to, and is about to abandon the party and the principles upon which it was raised to power. In short, the schemes of the K. G. C. to overthrow the Government, embrace the whole catalogue of strategy known to corrupt politicians.

4. FOREIGN INFLUENCE.—The K. G. C. are known to each other by secret signs and words. They seldom trust any documents to the mails, but keep messengers constantly in the field carrying information from one "Castle" (or "Club," "Lodge," "Society," &c.,) to another. (The term "Castle" is the proper designation of the place where "Knights" congregate to concoct treason.) There is the most perfect and uninterrupted communication between the South and England through this order. Their principal avenue is through the Canadas, where they have numerous "Castles" and co-workers, as well as in Europe. There are numerous Southerners located in Canada as connecting links in the agency, and several of the employees of the Provincial railroads, connecting with the States, are the active agents and "messengers" of this secret treason against the Government. At both ends of the Grand Trunk, the Great Western, the Buffalo and Lake Huron roads, those agents are busy, but mostly so on the Grand Trunk, and the connecting lines into Vermont. Several of the representatives of large British capitalists residing in Canada are known to be most active operators and sympathizers. The Donneganna and St. Lawrence hotels at Montreal are the resorts of Southern rebels, where they are met and treated with great kindness and cordiality; also at Quebec, Toronto, Hamilton, &c. The K. G. C. claim to own, or have a controlling interest in, nearly every leading newspaper in the Canadas. In Canada, as in England, this organization, and sympathy with the rebellion, is confined to the feudal, aristocratic, and what they *claim* to be, the *ruling* classes, viz: those "born to rule by royal prerogative." They dread the influence of Republican America; they consider her a rival power, dangerous to the extension of their own lease of monarchical rule, and are ready to seize upon the first favorable opportunity to assist in her overthrow—and thus demonstrate to their own subjects, already *restless*, if not clamorous, for many "reforms" approximating to our young Government, that the "model Republic" is a failure; that Democracy cannot constitute a permanent government, that nothing short of a monarchical, or strong central government, can withstand the shocks of ages. The overthrow, or division and disruption of our government, would be pointed to as a fulfillment of the long-heralded prophesies of monarchists. The active and adroit diplomacy of the rebel States, through their ablest men, knew well where to secure a strong foot-hold in Europe, and they struck with success. They sought the association of aristocracy and capital, as the strong point to be gained, and hence, to a large extent, have secured the tone of the aristocratic press, without striking the responsive chord in the hearts of the great mass of the European people—the working and tax-paying classes, whose representatives are "reformers"—those who turn a listening ear to the musical strains of liberty and equality which float to them from across the Atlantic, and cause the inquiry why they cannot enjoy the same blessing without risking a perilous voyage from their native land to the New World, where all are "sovereigns," and the rulers only the subjects and servants. The K. G. C. never seem to lack money to send messengers on long journeys, and keep them constantly in the field, or do anything else they deem important. This gives color to their claim that the European associated aristocracy are secretly furnishing large sums of money to second the base objects of the Southern rebellion. *I have no doubt of it.*

5. THE LAST RESORT—CIVIL WAR—ASSASSINATION!—But the most damnable and atrocious part of this dark plot is yet to be told, and if it does not arouse the languid patriotic blood now resting in security to stand united against the working of this foul treason, then, indeed, our liberties are in danger. The K. G. C., through this secret organization, have the blood-thirsty scheme of *assassinating* Northern Union men, and creating anarchy and civil war in the North, as a means of ending resistance to the rebellion! Believing that other means will fail, they are already privately armed and arming for the conflict.

I have before stated as a part of the programme, that all Northern Union men who voted for Lincoln, or *sustain the Government* in a vigorous prosecution of the war to crush out the rebellion, are to be branded "ABOLITIONISTS," *ergo*, "traitors," equally guilty with Jeff. Davis and his crew, *because* Garrison and Wendell Phillips and other fanatical Abolitionists, have been notorious and ignominious as *disunionists*. "Let the Northern Abolition traitors and the Southern Rebel leaders be hung up together, if at all," is now the watch-word.—" Let them perish in equal numbers, as the *authors* of the war."—" The Abolitionists of the North must first be *'put down*' before the war can come to an end."—"The danger of a Northern uprising against the Government, if the war is not *speedily* brought to a close."—"We are fighting our own brethren."—" They are willing to *compromise*, but the Abolitionists will not."—"The people will rise and fight before they will pay taxes to keep our soldiers killing our brothers in the South."—" The Abolitionists are worse traitors, and more to blame than the South."—" The Abolitionists must be cleaned out, and then we can have peace."—" The people must rise and hang the Abolitionists at the same time the army put down the rebellion South."—"Blood must flow in the North, as well as the South, before we get rid of the worst traitors to the Union." " Abolitionists must be put in Fort Warren as well as Southern men, if you want peace." These and numerous other similar dark and blood-foreboding expressions that may be heard in talking with high " Knights," only go to fully corroborate the written evidence now before me, of a blood-thirsty plot to assassinate Union men to "secure the success of the South." I have seen and read the special despatches of high " Knights," sent from one castle to the high officials of another, in which the whole programme of operations, and the means to be used were elaborately laid down and commented upon, in which it is always distinctly stated that the only way to success in the North, is to secure the *success of the South* by a concerted action throughout the North—that the country must be tired and worried out with taxes and the horrors of war, until a pretense is given to warrant a Northern civil war, and an uprising against the "Abolitionists," as the cause of the beginning and continuance of the conflict. Then the private arms are to be used. Each K. G. C. is pledged to arm himself with a long knife and a revolving pistol. They are also provided with small dark pocket or police lamps. One dispatch to a high functionary, stated that if secresy and success attended the project—and he had no doubt on that score—it would prove a second Sicilian Vesper, which has reference also, to some of the test words of recognition. " Are you going to Vespers ?"—" Are you ready for Vespers ?" is the sly way of asking each other if they are " *armed*" and " *ready* ;" and also of asking a stranger if he is a K. G. C.—or, if in a mixed crowd, any conversation in which the word " Vespers" is used, indicates membership, which leads to further tests.

I have heard the more desperate openly state that if this war is not closed in less than four months, " Abolition" blood would flow in every Northern city. I am not permitted to go more into detail at this time. I have given you but a faint outline of the plot, and the means to be used to overthrow the old Ship of State. When it culminates into the assassination of Union men in the peaceful, loyal North, by a band of secretly organized traitors—when the bell shall toll for another Sicilian Vespers—when traitors shall shout their songs of rebellion as the signal for the Grand Carnival of Treason to commence, with one side secretly armed for the conflict—then the country will inquire with amazement, whether the events of March 30, 1282, are not to have their counterpart here, in the year 1862, for no other crime than being loyal to the Government, and wishing to put down the most wicked and causeless rebellion that ever existed! Then, perhaps, the Government will be aroused to the importance of not harboring vipers in its bosom to sting its very life-blood—then the loyal people will rise in their might and protect their own liberties, and woe be unto those who have their lot cast with the K. G. C., or have followed their leadership.

These are startling developments, and will be vigorously hooted down by every K. G. C. who is true to his obligations. Let it be so for the present. There are some among them who have yet an inkling of patriotism left, and cannot, and will not be bound to this wicked conspiracy. It is to this source that you are indebted for the facts above stated—facts, which I will say to you, may be most implicitly relied upon, and the time will arrive when what I have stated, will be verified, and much of the same character added to it. At some future time, developments will be made that will satisfy you that I am no *alarmist*, and men high in the confidence of the people will be so connected with this secret treason, that the country will despise their memory. In the mean time, let every loyal man, *wherever he is*, be watchful and vigilant for the signs that I have indicated, to identify and mark the sure enemies of the Union, and in most cases the sure trade-marks of the K. G. C. Their emissaries are busy and on the move. The organization is extensive, penetrating the back woods and the plains. In many cases, in remote places, one, two, or three trusted members, are all who are entrusted with the secrets, but *they* are busy in making and controling opinion—in *educating* their partisans up to the proper point. The New York " Caucassian" newspaper, sustained by a private fund of the order, is the *special* organ of the " Castles." The principal head quarters in the North, are Philadelphia, New York City and Cincinnati. They have a large number of small newspaper editors in their secrets, some of which have to be checked occasionally for too plain talk.

While the "Caucassian" is the *special* organ, and privately circulated in many places, there are many leading newspapers in the North, said to be edited by "Knights," and eagerly sought for by the brotherhood in their respective States, and in different States, to indicate the progress of the work, and which are deemed able auxiliaries. Among them I may mention the *Herald, Journal of Commerce, Express* and a French newspaper, New York City; the *Courier* and the *Post*, Boston; the *Times*, Hartford; the *Atlas* and *Argus*, Albany; the *Union*, Rochester; the *Courier*, Buffalo; the *Enquirer*, Cincinnati; the *Free Press*, Detroit; the *Times*. Chicago; the *News*, Milwaukee, and many others of less note. These are the principal names on the lists of traveling messengers for those States.

I have extended this communication to a far greater length than I had intended, but I could not well make it shorter and do the subject justice. I submit it for your consideration, believing that you will discover many things in your State and vicinity to corroborate what I have said. The work of the K. G. C., as used here, is revised and changed from that used six months ago in the Southern States. In the first degree, but little of its real character is divulged. It is simply represented as a "Society to oppose Abolitionists." Little by little the candidate is led into the vortex of treason. *I earnestly warn all good men against taking the first step.*

Yours very truly, *for the whole Union,*   ※※※

Fellow Citizens—Loyal Union-loving men of the United States! What think you of these things? We have proved, upon testimony which you cannot reasonably doubt, the presence in your very midst, of a *deadly conspiracy* which threatens your liberties, your rights as citizens, and even the existence of that Union which you so highly prize. And yet the half has not been told. There are other secrets of the K. G. C. yet to be revealed. These secrets are in the possession of those whose duty it is, and who have the power to punish the traitors who compose the organization; and if they do not perform that duty, we intend to make further disclosures. For the present we must forbear.

That foul disease which traitors, thirty years ago, fastened upon the body politic, has grown to the proportions of a cancer of the most dangerous character. *It must be eradicated*, or you will yet have occasion to mourn over the wreck of all your long-cherished hopes of your country's greatness and glory. Traitors at home, leagued with enemies abroad, even now present the knife at the heart of your bleeding country. Corruption, rank and poisonous, faithlessness and treachery in high places, disregard of the most sacred obligations of man to his fellow man and to his God, have borne their legitimate fruits. Treason stalks unblushingly through the land. Artful, intriguing politicians and unprincipled demagogues have brought your noble Government to the verge of destruction.

Your patriotic fathers, through much of personal suffering, and untold sacrifices of blood and treasure, laid broad and deep, cemented in blood and baptized in tears, the foundations of this glorious fabric of free government, fondly cherishing the hope that it would stand to remotest ages, an asylum for the oppressed of all nations, a beacon for the weary victims of tyranny, and a terror to the despotisms of the Old World. This priceless legacy *must be preserved*. We cannot believe that you will prove recreant to your country, to posterity, and to God. We believe that the blood and treasure so freely expended in the suppression of the atrocious rebellion now rapidly reeling to its final doom, will bear yet more fruit—that you are ready yet again, if need be, to offer your lives and all that you possess, for the preservation of your Government, and for its establishment upon a basis so solid that it shall stand as a monument of human wisdom, and as the great bulwark of Christianity, Civilization, and true Liberty, until time shall be no more!

These last lines are penned and our little work goes to press amid the rejoicings of a great nation over the prospect of a speedy and enduring peace. And while our pæans ascend to Heaven, let us extend to our misguided brethren of the South the hand of friendship and brotherly love. We may now confidently hope for a lasting peace to our distracted country, and that the jealousies and heart-burnings which have so long rankled like a festering ulcer, and made bitter enemies of those who never should have been other than friends, may be forever lost and forgotten. The Great Rebellion will soon be numbered among the things of the past. And now let us of the North and of the South, of the East and of the West, burying past differences and trusting in God for the future, join hearts and hands in the earnest resolve that neither dissensions at home nor aggressions from abroad shall henceforth hinder the onward march of the Great Republic!

[Intentionally Left Blank]

[Intentionally Left Blank]

[Intentionally Left Blank]

[Intentionally Left Blank]

[Intentionally Left Blank]

[Intentionally Left Blank]

[Intentionally Left Blank]

[Intentionally Left Blank]

Printed in Poland
by Amazon Fulfillment
Poland Sp. z o.o., Wrocław